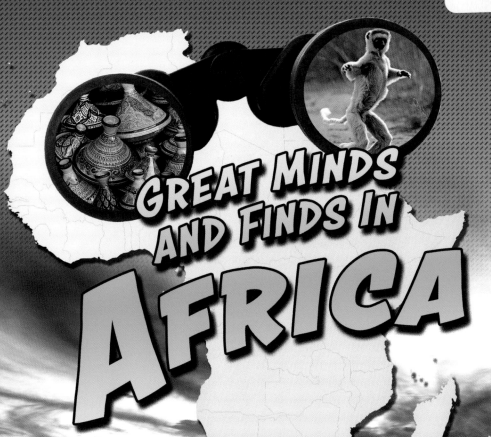

# GREAT MINDS AND FINDS IN AFRICA

Mike Downs

Rourke
Educational Media

A Division of
Carson
Dellosa
Education

Bridges

# BEFORE AND DURING READING ACTIVITIES

## Before Reading: *Building Background Knowledge and Vocabulary*

Building background knowledge can help children process new information and build upon what they already know. Before reading a book, it is important to tap into what children already know about the topic. This will help them develop their vocabulary and increase their reading comprehension.

### Questions and Activities to Build Background Knowledge:

1. Look at the front cover of the book and read the title. What do you think this book will be about?
2. What do you already know about this topic?
3. Take a book walk and skim the pages. Look at the table of contents, photographs, captions, and bold words. Did these text features give you any information or predictions about what you will read in this book?

### Vocabulary: *Vocabulary Is Key to Reading Comprehension*

Use the following directions to prompt a conversation about each word.

- Read the vocabulary words.
- What comes to mind when you see each word?
- What do you think each word means?

**Vocabulary Words:**

- apartheid
- artifacts
- canals
- conservationists
- glacier
- hieroglyphics
- migration
- pneumonia
- poaching
- rural

## During Reading: *Reading for Meaning and Understanding*

To achieve deep comprehension of a book, children are encouraged to use close reading strategies. During reading, it is important to have children stop and make connections. These connections result in deeper analysis and understanding of a book.

 Close Reading a Text

During reading, have children stop and talk about the following:

- Any confusing parts
- Any unknown words
- Text to text, text to self, text to world connections
- The main idea in each chapter or heading

Encourage children to use context clues to determine the meaning of any unknown words. These strategies will help children learn to analyze the text more thoroughly as they read.

When you are finished reading this book, turn to the next-to-last page for **Text-Dependent Questions** and an **Extension Activity**.

# TABLE OF CONTENTS

# WHERE IN THE WORLD IS AFRICA?

Africa is the world's second largest continent, making up about one-fifth of Earth's land area. More than 50 countries are within its borders. Africa is surrounded by two seas and two oceans.

Adventure through Africa and learn about the people, ideas, and inventions that have come from this incredible place.

*The Twelve Apostles mountain range near Cape Town, South Africa, has 12 peaks.*

## Africa by the Numbers

**Population:** >1.33 billion

**Size:** >11.72 million square miles or >30.3 million square kilometers

**Highest Point:** Mount Kilimanjaro, >19,340 feet or 5,895 meters

# NATURAL WONDERS

Africa has many different natural environments. Blazing hot sands in the Sahara Desert and tropical rainforests are both found on this continent. Mount Kilimanjaro even has a **glacier** at its top!

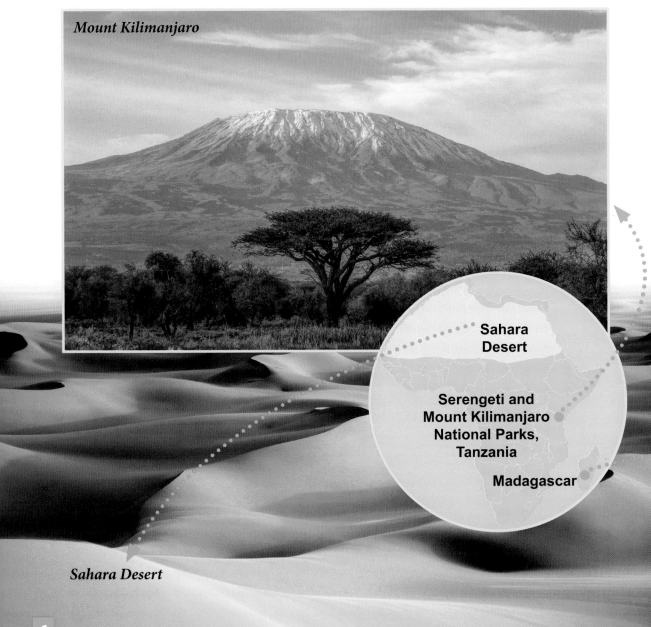

*Mount Kilimanjaro*

Sahara Desert

Serengeti and Mount Kilimanjaro National Parks, Tanzania

Madagascar

*Sahara Desert*

*There are two rainy seasons per year in the Serengeti.*

Unique living things help make Africa such an incredible place. Giant trees, huge ferns, and beautiful flowers can be found around the continent. Lions, elephants, and giraffes roam the Serengeti grassland. It even has the largest wildebeest **migration** on the planet. Scientists come from around the world to study the land and living things of Africa.

## Noisy Neighbors

The island of Madagascar, off the coast of Africa, is the only place in the world with wild lemurs. These small relatives of monkeys and apes cluck, grunt, chirp like birds, or even howl like an airhorn.

# ANCIENT ORIGINS

Africa is famous for fossils. Ancient living things have been found all over the continent. One of the most famous of these is the skeleton called Lucy. Lucy is an example of a relative of modern humans that lived about 3.2 million years ago. The discovery in the country of Ethiopia changed how many scientists thought about human history.

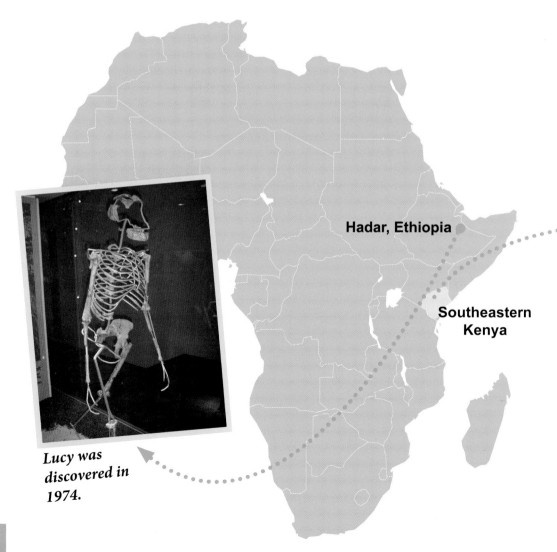

Hadar, Ethiopia

Southeastern Kenya

*Lucy was discovered in 1974.*

Fossils and **artifacts** can be very valuable. They are frequently stolen and sold. Dr. George Abungu, a scientist from the country of Kenya, works to stop this. He has written about missing African artifacts. This has led to the return of grave markers and other important African treasures.

*Dr. Abungu was made a knight by the country of France for his work in protecting African history.*

*Vigango grave markers can be up to nine feet (2.7 meters) high.*

# CANALS AND CROPS

Cities need farms to grow enough food for the people living there. The ancient Egyptians developed farming along the Nile River in Africa by building **canals**. The food they produced let Egyptians build huge cities.

Modern farmers use computers to help grow crops. Programs such as those from the Nigerian company Zenvus can collect information about soil using computers. That information can help farmers decide if they need to change anything.

*Many of the ancient artificial canals in Egypt still exist.*

*Farmers can use computers to control how much water their crops get.*

## Secret Canals

Cape Town in the country of South Africa has canals hidden underneath the city. They were blocked by bricks when the canals became polluted in the 1800s.

# BUILDING BIG!

Sir David Frank Adjaye was born in Dar es Salaam in the country of Tanzania. He uses his experience as a young person in Africa when he designs buildings. He has become famous around the world and has designed buildings such as the National Museum of African American History and Culture in Washington, DC. He wrote a series of books about African architecture to teach the world more about the continent's incredible buildings.

The pyramids in Egypt may be Africa's most famous buildings. The biggest one had about 2.3 million stones. Each stone weighed approximately 2,000 pounds (907 kilograms). Builders did not have modern machines to help lift the heavy stones. Instead, the builders probably slid the stones across the sand on a sled.

*The National Museum of African American History and Culture is wrapped in a layer of metal.*

*The Great Pyramid of Giza is one of the seven wonders of the ancient world. It is surrounded by several other, smaller pyramids.*

Giza, Egypt

Dar es Salaam, Tanzania

## To the Sky

The Great Pyramid of Giza was thought to be the tallest building in the world for a long time. In 2019, the tallest building in the world was the Burj Khalifa. This giant tower in Dubai, United Arab Emirates, is 2,722 feet (829.8 meters) tall. It is so large that it has more than 24,000 windows.

# WRITING AND MATH

Writing and math are important in every civilization. They help us learn and invent new things. Africa has some of the earliest known writing, called **hieroglyphics**. This is a system of small pictures that work similar to an alphabet. These pictures are frequently found in ancient Egyptian writing and buildings.

Africa is also home to the oldest known mathematical object, the Lebombo bone. It is over 43,000 years old. Some scientists think that it might have been used as a calendar.

*Ancient Egyptian writing was sometimes found on papyrus, a material similar to thick paper.*

*You can tell which way to read hieroglyphics by the direction that they face. If the pictures face left, the hieroglyphics are read from left to right. If they face right, they are read from right to left.*

## A Modern Memory

The Bibliotheca Alexandrina in Alexandria, Egypt, is a huge library and art center. It was built in part to honor an ancient Egyptian library that was destroyed. The Bibliotheca Alexandrina has space for about eight million books.

# MOVE IT!

*The Suez Canal made a shorter route for ships, which saved both time and money.*

Suez, Egypt

Kikwit, Democratic Republic of the Congo

Travel is important for trade. The ancient Egyptians traded along the Nile River and Mediterranean Sea. They did this using large wooden boats, but some trips were very long. In 1869, the Suez Canal was built in Egypt. It connects the

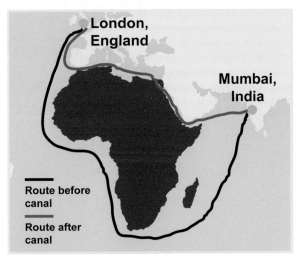

*The shorter path through the Suez Canal also brought trade to different parts of Africa.*

Mediterranean Sea and the Red Sea. Using the Suez Canal can shorten a boat's journey by 4,300 miles (7,000 kilometers).

Travel by land is getting easier thanks to a scientist from Kikwit in the Democratic Republic of the Congo, Dr. Ngalula Sandrine Mubenga. She has invented a way to make batteries in electric cars last much longer. In places where not much gasoline is available, electric cars make it easier to get supplies such as food and services such as healthcare.

*Ngalula Sandrine Mubenga now works to encourage young engineers.*

# PROTECTING NATURE

The plant and animal life of Africa was important to Kenyan activist Dr. Wangari Muta Maathai. She started a program called the Green Belt Movement. She worked to stop the unnecessary cutting of trees. She also encouraged people, especially women, to plant more trees. She received the Nobel Peace Prize in 1977. She was the first African woman to win this prize.

*Muta Maathai*

Modern **conservationists** use technology to keep animals from being hunted illegally. Scientists set up a protection system near Kruger National Park in South Africa. Computers keep track of animals as well as anyone entering or exiting the area. Because of this system, the scientists have nearly stopped rhinoceros **poaching** in the area.

**Kruger National Park**

*Conservationists in Kenya feed elephants whose parents were killed or separated from them.*

## An Incredible Recovery

In the early 1900s, only between 50 and 100 white rhinos were left alive in the wild. Many people worked to protect them. In 2019, it was estimated that almost 19,000 white rhinos could be alive in the wild.

*Wari is played on the same board as mancala but has different rules.*

# FUN AND GAMES

Do you like to play games? You might have played one that started in Africa! Mancala involves moving small stones or other markers around two rows of small holes. The game may be as old as ancient Egypt and is still popular in modern times. It has been turned into other forms such as wari.

The game of horseshoes likely came from the South African game of jukskei. Small pieces of wood are thrown at a peg. Teams score points by knocking over the peg.

Around Africa, computer experts are setting up projects and offices to help new technology get made. Kenyan expert Lilian Nduati wants to help other African people make more video games. She thinks that people can use video games to tell stories that their families have told for hundreds of years. Video games can help keep these stories alive.

*Video games help people have fun and connect with friends.*
*They can also be used to tell important stories.*

# STAYING HEALTHY

When someone is sick, doctors sometimes mistake one illness for another. This is often the case with **pneumonia**, which can be deadly if not treated. A team of scientists in Uganda designed a special jacket, the MamaOpe, that can help doctors decide if a person has pneumonia. It sends health information to an app, making it easy for a doctor to review the information.

*Brian Turyabagye (left) and Besufekad Shifferaw (right) display the MamaOpe jacket.*

Fresh water is important for staying healthy and clean. It can be difficult to get enough clean water to **rural** areas in Africa far from rivers or lakes. The Hippo Water Roller was invented by South African engineers Pettie Petzer and Johan Jonker. A person using a Hippo Water Roller can move five times more water than they could by carrying it. This means people have more access to fresh water and better health.

*The water in this Hippo Roller weighs 198 pounds (90 kilograms).*

Africa has a history of great minds in surgery. The Edwin Smith papyrus is a a piece of ancient Egyptian writing discovered in Luxor, Egypt. It discusses 48 surgical cases and explains treatment. This was long before many people knew what surgery was!

There are not many female surgeons in Africa, but Dr. Lindiwe Sidali wanted to change that. She became the first female heart and lung surgeon in South Africa. She has even worked on an all-woman surgical team. She works hard to inspire others, especially girls and women, in medicine and health.

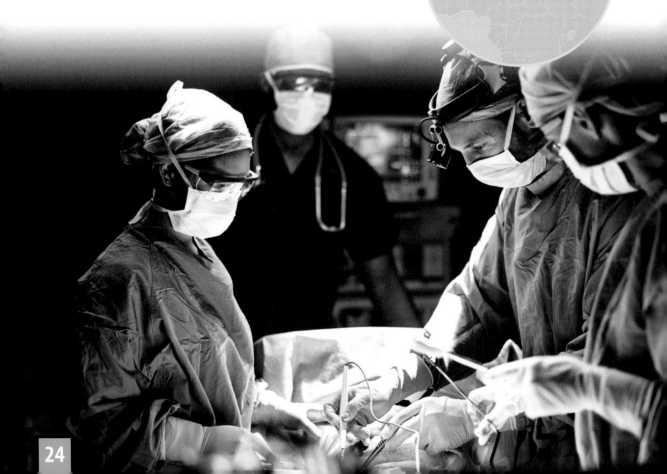

Luxor, Egypt

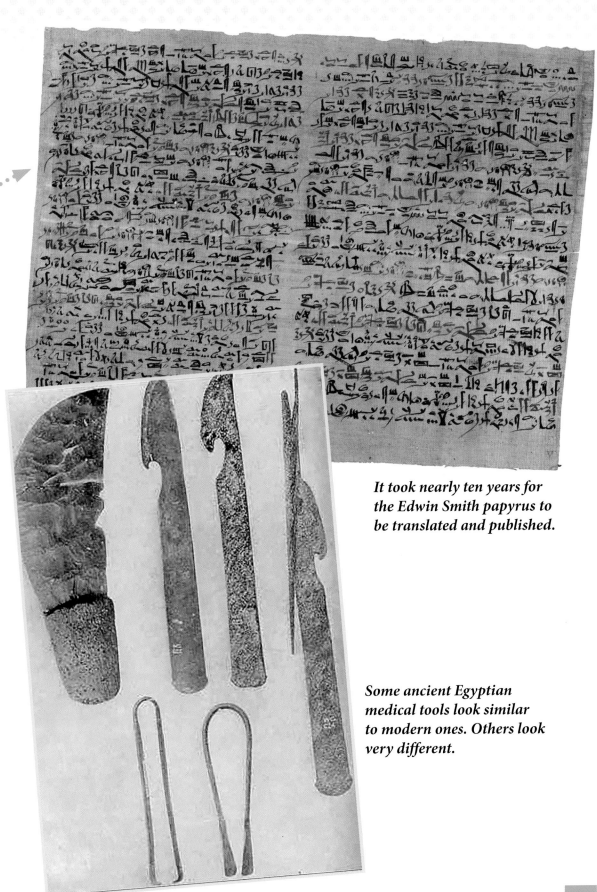

*It took nearly ten years for the Edwin Smith papyrus to be translated and published.*

*Some ancient Egyptian medical tools look similar to modern ones. Others look very different.*

# WORKING FOR FREEDOM

Until the early 1990s, South Africa and South West Africa had racist government systems called **apartheid**. Activists around the world worked to end apartheid. Desmond Tutu is a South African activist who led churches to support anti-apartheid causes. He also worked for women to be accepted as church leaders, for equality among all people, and for human rights.

*Desmond Tutu has written seven books.*

Nelson Mandela worked with Desmond Tutu to end apartheid. Mandela was put in prison in 1962 for trying to overthrow South Africa's unfair government. He became South Africa's first black head of state. After retiring as president of South Africa, he worked to end poverty and improve healthcare in Africa.

"It always seems impossible until it's done."

-Nelson Mandela

*Nelson Mandela served 27 years in prison before becoming South Africa's head of state.*

## Prizes for Peace

Both Desmond Tutu and Nelson Mandela won the Nobel Peace Prize, among other awards. Mandela himself received more than 250 honors.

# INCREDIBLE AFRICA

Africa has a rich history and a bright future. Its story is full of great minds and fantastic finds. How would your life be different without them?

**Democratic Republic of Congo**

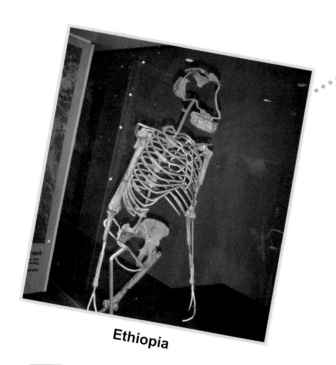
**Ethiopia**

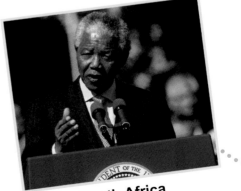
**South Africa**